MW00438448

Angie Smith

# Habits of the Happiest Teachers

24 STRATEGIES TO INCREASE INTENTIONALITY,
STREAMLINE YOUR WORKLOAD, AND
PRODUCE LASTING JOY.

For
Matt, Kaylie, and Chase.
My dreams are big because of you.
Thank you for always encouraging me
and being my biggest cheerleaders.
I love you.

# Contents

# Introduction

**Welcome to the world of education:**

**Right now you...**

... feel like more continues to be added to your already "full teacher plate", or

... don't feel you have the capacity to get it all done and are burning out, or

... wish your students were more engaged in their learning.

**You find teaching to be...**

... overwhelming with too many demands and moving parts, or

... less teaching and more managing the ever changing environment of a classroom, curriculums and behaviors, or

... not what you signed up for.

**You want strategies...**

... that teach you to manage your time and eliminate what is not important, and

... help you accomplish what needs to get done in a systematic way without having to stay late or come early, and

... build solid relationships with your students that practically eliminate unwanted behaviors, and

... teach you how to carve out time that truly rests and refuels you (guilt free).

If you are feeling any or ALL of this, you are in the right place.

Hi! I am Angie, a Washington State teacher of 20+ years, who is passionate about helping teachers like you eliminate burnout and bring the JOY back to our noble profession! Over the last 10 years, I have worked to transform my own teaching life into a life I LOVE by adding intentional automation and organization into specific areas of high need. Now they run themselves and I have time for what I love to do.

*I haven't always been a happy teacher. Five years ago, I was 2 years back into a full time teaching job after 10 years of teaching half time, having babies, raising littles, and attempting to be a good wife, daughter, sister and friend all at the same time. My hubby, who is also a teacher, was by my side burning the candle at both ends too so to speak. Teaching kids and coming home to kids the same age was almost more than we could handle. We loved it- the teaching and our babies- but we were tired. No scratch that. We were EXHAUSTED. Something had to give, and I was searching.*

*That was when I stumbled upon a class written by one of my all-time favorite teacher authors, Angela Watson, called the 40 Hour Teacher Workweek. (FYI, you should take this class! Look her up and check it out! It is life giving!) That title alone had my attention! So I used what little extra money I had left from my teacher's salary and took this year-long online course, and slowly but surely, week by week, I changed my life into something I LOVE.*

*I began to add systems and strategies at school and learned to be the most productive version of myself there. I made my classroom more "self-running," delegated jobs to kids and found a place for everything. I used my time more efficiently. I learned to designate time to plan every week, used my prep time to grade, and had lunch* *with my teacher friends to connect and give my mind a break. I protected my before and after school time by not stopping to chat and by keeping my door closed if I needed to get something done. I also learned that I could not do everything. I said no to extra committees and extra assignments. I got rid of the good and only taught and gave time to the **great**.*

*By changing the way I worked at school, I was able to create more time at home for the ones I love. I began to "leave it all at school" and give my full attention to my family when I was there. I also began to let some of these systems spill over into my home life. I began to meal plan, I started a morning routine, and I began to create time for the activities I love the most so that I could rest, recharge and be ready for the work that lay ahead the following week.*

*Many of the small changes, systems, and strategies that originated when I took the 40 Hour Teacher Workweek Course have changed my life forever and that is why I am writing this book. I want to share with you how I have adapted to make them work for me and how they have changed my teaching for the better. My hope is that you might use a strategy or two from this book to lighten your load or shift your perspective. Ultimately, I want to help you find your unique true happiness all while continuing to teach.*

This book is broken down into 3 parts; ways to streamline your **home** life, how to make your **classroom** work for you, and easily upping your **self-care** game so that you can be present and engaged for the ones you love.

By picking up this book, you have already expressed that you are ready for a change. I am beyond excited to work alongside you and join you on a journey of personal transformation and self-reflection that will ultimately pay dividends of happiness, peacefulness and contentment in your teaching career and your life.

Let's get started.

# Part 1:

## Streamline Your Home Life

"*You deserve to be happy.
You deserve to live a life you
are excited about.*"

*– unknown*

# Chapter 1: The Why

When Sunday afternoon rolls around, how do you feel? Do you love your job? Are you excited for a new week? Do you love where you work, what you do, the difference you are making?

Or are you dreading it? Every. Single. Minute. Of it?

Most people dread their day job because of one of these 3 main reasons. One, they feel underappreciated and not valued. Two, the environment is negative. Or three, they don't feel safe to take healthy risks. If you are in a teaching job where you are feeling this way and one of these three reasons is why, it may be time to make a move to a new location. This may not be the place for you. You may or may not be doing something new, or you just may need a change of venue.

But, what if those reasons aren't why you don't like going to work every day? What if you just can't pinpoint why you are unhappy? You find yourself in the mundane trap of going through the motions of your everyday life. You do the bare minimum, don't challenge yourself, and more or less just get through the day clinging to the weekend which now comes and goes faster than ever.

Well, if this is where you find yourself, you may need to zero in on WHY you are here in the first place. This thing you do for 8 hours a day, 5 days a week...WHY are you here? What is the driving force that put you here? Why did you travel down this road originally? Once you have that answer, it's time to focus on WHY you aren't happy. Again, you spend MOST of your time here, shouldn't you be happy?

The reason I ask you to do this is because it might be time for a perspective switch. You may need to go back to where you came from by placing your WHY front and center. No matter what, you need to get back to your why if you are unhappy. So much of how you feel about your job can be fixed in your mind using your perspective and attitude. When you get back to WHY you are here in the first place, it helps to reignite that passion and love for the work you are doing. It gives you purpose for being there.

Your WHY could even be that this J.O.B. is a means to an end. It is getting you from point A to point B so that you can eventually do the important work that you are on this earth to do in the first place. Even then, it's important to identify that, so that you can truly be happy where you are, in this moment, as you move toward the future.

So stop now. Zero in on your WHY. Make sure you know exactly what it is and that it is crystal clear. When you have it... keep reading!

My WHY! I am in this particular job because _____

_____

_____

_____

_____

_____

_____

_____

Ok! Now that you remember WHY you are working in this field, at this job, in this career, it's time to reexamine your ATTITUDE.

How do you come to work every morning? Are you there to "Bring the Joy?" Is your attitude positive and energetic? You don't realize it, but you have the power to change the environment with your attitude. People are drawn to positive people, and the thing is, they become more positive when you are more positive. Attitude is a funny thing. You may have to dig down deep and force it out for a while, but then it will become habit, just like anything else, and you will begin to feel happy inside as a result.

After that, check in to see if you are looking for your job to satisfy you, or if you are working to grow where you are. Are you there to do the bare minimum, or are you searching for ways to challenge yourself, contribute and give back to your company or school? If you are coming to work doing the smallest amount just to get by, your mental state is such and you will NEVER find satisfaction with your work.

Is this work TRULY something you enjoy? Is it the best way possible to ultimately achieve a life you love? If it is, you will make the best of where you are. You will choose to grow where you are planted. You will change your mindset to, "What can I do better?" You will ask yourself, "What can I do to make our school better?"

Friends, this life is short and you are never permanently stuck. If you are truly unhappy in your work, it might be time to make a change (or think about making a change) whether it be mentally or physically. But hear this, YOU DESERVE TO BE HAPPY. The thing is, sometimes you have to work at it. Happiness doesn't just appear. You have to look for it and reach for it by finding JOY in the small things, the ordinary, the everyday.

## Action Steps:

1. Identify WHY you chose this profession in the first place. You can use your answer from before, but write down everything you can possibly think of that brought you to this career.

_____

_____

_____

_____

_____

_____

_____

2.  Are you happy teaching in this place? YES or NO

3.  If YES, skip to action step 5.

4.  If No, is the reason you are unhappy in this profession related to the location (atmosphere, underappreciated, not safe to take healthy risks)? If so, you may need to make a location change.

_____

_____

_____

_____

_____

_____

5.  How's your attitude as you enter school every day? Be honest. Do you ooze positivity, daily? Or do you really have to work to be positive?

_____

_____

_____

_____

_____

_____

_____

If you really have to work to be positive, it may be time for an attitude adjustment. There may be other things in your life that are pulling you to this place. Keep reading. This book is packed with strategies that can help you get more organized and less stressed so that you can be positive and genuinely happy when you enter your classroom every single day.

"*Acknowledging
the good
that you already have in your
life
is the foundation
for all abundance.*"

–Eckhart Tolle

# Chapter 2: Finding JOY When You Are Burned Out

I t's hard to be happy when the norm is "how many things can I fit into this day?" There are pressures from home and pressures from work. Then on top of that, we continue to overload and compare ourselves with the Pinterest teacher or the Magnolia home. We wonder why we don't feel joyful when we cram all we can into each and every waking hour. We wonder why we come home feeling burned out, down, grumpy and tired.

The dictionary says that JOY is a feeling of great pleasure and happiness. Joy is healthy, joy relieves stress, joy heals, joy feels good, joy inspires, joy motivates, but MOST importantly, joy begets joy and connects us to others.

So how do we get joy? Where do we find it? Well, if you really think about it...

Joy is a CHOICE!

Joy begins and grows with one thing...gratitude.

I came to a point in life a long time ago where I chose to consciously choose JOY every day. It is SO unbelievably sad to me to hear people when asked how they are, respond glumly and say in a sad, sarcastic tone, "Livin' the dream."

It is NAILS ON A CHALKBOARD to me, people!

I want to just shake them and say, "If you don't like your life, change it!" YOU are in control of YOUR life. And if you aren't happy, it is YOUR responsibility to find out why and make it better.

Even on my darkest days when teacher burnout is at its greatest, there is SOMETHING to be grateful for. And don't get me wrong, I have bad days. I will complain at times when things are a mess. But not EVERYDAY. I work hard to make sure that that is not my normal. And one way I do this is with a gratefulness practice. When you are grateful, it is impossible to be down. Please hear me, IMPOSSIBLE! But, it's up to you to choose how you will feel gratitude. You need to find a way to do it daily.

Here is a practice I use:

Grab a journal. It doesn't need to be anything special. A simple $.99 spiral notebook will do. Now open it up and make a list of 10 things every day. I do this during my morning routine, but you could do it anytime. The trick with this, I have learned from a mentor of mine, Rachel Hollis, is not to choose the big things like my family, my marriage, or my house. If you begin by using these things, you'll run out fast or repeat the same things over and over, and your gratitude journal will have little effect.

Instead, choose 10 little things that have happened in the last 24 hours, like the thank you note that was placed on your desk today, or the compliment someone gave you in the hall at work.

When you practice gratitude in this way, you begin to see the world in a grateful light, and happiness is hard to deny.

So actually, it's pretty easy to begin to CHOOSE joy even when you are in the midst of teacher burnout. You begin by taking a step back, slowing down, and being present. Then, in that moment, you choose to be grateful for what you have, who you are, and the little things around you. By thinking and acting gratefully, you FEEL joy. And the BEST part about it is when you feel joy, you SPREAD joy!

I know it might seem impossible, but there are an infinite number of simple things you can pick from every day that will help bring joy into your world, and help you spread it to others, if you are willing. So are you willing? It's ultimately up to you.

## Action Steps:

1.  If you are ready to take this step and release teacher burnout for good, you are in the right place! Feel free to download my FREE Gratitude Journal at www.thisorganizedteacherlife.com in the RESOURCES section, or grab any notebook you have lying around.

2.  Start today! Write 10 things you are grateful for. It takes less than 5 minutes to begin changing the way you think forever!

# Reflect!

Today, I am grateful for...

1. _____

2. _____

3. _____

4. _____

5. _____

6. _____

7. _____

8. _____

9. _____

10. _____

*"With organization comes empowerment."*

*– Lynda Peterson*

# Chapter 3: The Power of a List

When it comes to staying focused and on track, I struggle. I don't know about you, but I find myself flitting from one thing to another all day long, putting off this and that until I have done MANY things that Don't. Even. Matter. And the important things STILL aren't done!

The biggest part of this is, time after time, I am FEELING like I never get anything done. Day after day, I would be exhausted at home and at school. It's not that I am not doing task after task, but I am feeling empty, as if all of my effort is going unnoticed and just being funneled into an empty abyss, not adding to my life or the lives of the ones I love.

I needed to find a way to get my important things done, not ALL the things, but the Most. Important. Things. And I needed to FEEL the accomplishment. I needed to see and be able to say, "Look what I have done today!" and know that I absolutely accomplished what I needed to get done.

Enter, My Evolving List!

The one thing that has absolutely SAVED me when it comes to this predicament is My Evolving List. I know. I know. It sounds too simple. Everybody uses a list. Well, this is just a little twist on an old favorite that originated with teacher-mentor, Angela Watson.

It has made a monumental difference in my life, and it goes a little something like this.

- ★ Find a piece of paper or use notes in your phone. (I like to use a large notepad of really thick, beautiful paper. I purchased mine through Dapperdesk at emilyley.com.)

★ Brainstorm all of the things that you would like to get done today, and then put them on your list in order of importance.

- Some of us prefer to leave things out of order of importance and pick and choose throughout the day. If this is you, then do it that way. The important thing is that it gets done!

★ Now, begin your day. Get things done from your list as you go about your day. If it is on the top of your list, do THIS first.

★ As you get things done on your list, cross them off. (Yes, physically put a line through them!)

★ By the end of the day, you will have many things crossed off your list and feel an AMAZING sense of accomplishment looking at all of the items you erased from your life! Yay you!

Now... don't stop here! This is where the evolving comes into place!

Move to tomorrow...

Take the items that didn't get done. You are NOT a superhero. There will still be some things that become less important as you move through the week or other situations that come up and don't allow time for you to accomplish your WHOLE list. That's OK! Take the items that were left on your list and begin tomorrow's list! Rank them in a new order of importance for you to get done tomorrow. Repeat tomorrow what you did today! Do your most important things first and Cross. Them. Off! Feel the accomplishment rush through your veins, and enjoy that you are getting your most important things done and you can physically see and feel it.

Take YOUR LIST to the NEXT LEVEL:

★ Plan once a week and add to or reorganize daily.

★ Identify your BIG goals and get them done first. This only works if you put those big things on top of your list and get them done before all other tasks.

★ Group similar tasks. You will get more done if you can do all similar items together.

★ Build in a day to get those "once a week" tasks done, like going through the mail.

★ Avoid being overwhelmed by identifying tasks that you can say NO to or delegate to someone else. Also, be mindful of what you say YES to. World renowned author and speaker, Jen Hatmaker once said, "If it isn't a Hell YES, then it's a NO!" This saying always helps me to make that distinction.

★ Make time daily/weekly to rest and/or recharge. You can't continue to go at a crazy pace. Block out time to slow down and rest.

I keep a list on the corner of my desk at school and cross items off all week. It keeps me focused at school and helps me to not forget to send that quick email or get something prepared. All. The. Things. Are right in front of me, all of the time. Super helpful to my fleeting memory.

At home, I use a list in my notes on my phone. Same idea, just with me everywhere I go!

I hope you LOVE this system as much as I do and that it can help you get things done and FEEL the accomplishment of all you are doing every day!

# Action Steps:

1. Grab a notepad or designate where you are going to keep your list electronically OR start right here! I have added space below for you to begin.

2. Begin at the beginning of the week. Write down EVERYTHING you want to get done this week.

3. Rank them in order of importance. Most important at the top!

4. Get to work moving through that list as you go about your day.

5. The following morning, reorganize your list, moving things to the top of the priority list or eliminating them altogether.

6. Add your items for today, and get to work.

7. Whatever you do, make it your own, and let this system work for you!

# Reflect!

**Brainstorm** everything you want to get done this week.

_____
_____
_____
_____
_____
_____
_____
_____
_____
_____
_____
_____
_____
_____
_____
_____
_____
_____
_____

Now, **Rank** in order of importance! (Start at the top!)

_____
_____
_____
_____
_____
_____
_____
_____
_____
_____
_____
_____
_____
_____
_____
_____
_____
_____

*"Today only happens once. Make it AMAZING!"*

*—unknown*

# Chapter 4: A Morning Routine That Will Excite and Energize

Do you wake up grumpy? Do you struggle to get out of bed without hitting the snooze button over and over and over again? Are you ready to QUIT that behavior for good?

**I have a challenge for you! It's too good, but true!**

It might sound crazy, but WAKE. UP. EARLIER.

You may be saying, "WHAT, are you kidding me?!"

NOPE...I'm not kidding...Stay with me...

Set your alarm for 30-60 minutes earlier and wake up! BUT do something that is enjoyable to you. Make yourself a cup of coffee, tea, whatever makes you happy. Then, either grab an uplifting book, read your bible, stretch, meditate, work out, or grab a gratitude journal and write 10 things that you are grateful for right off the bat, first thing in the morning.

**ABSOLUTELY NO SOCIAL MEDIA! NO SOCIAL MEDIA! Yes, it's fun, but it steals your joy! (Not to mention your time)**

Then think about your day! Make your list, your lunch, whatever you need to be successful that day. Then, pour another cup and hop in the shower!

It seems crazy, but it ACTUALLY works! When you wake up, you are happy to make the coffee, read, or just have some time for you. AND you are planned and ready for your day. DOUBLE WIN! You aren't racing through the house at the last minute to do All. The. Things.

{QUICK ADD for the Night Owls}

If you are a night owl and this sounds HORRIBLE to you, think about switching it up. Do your "morning routine" just before bed. Maybe switch the coffee to decaf, but make the lunches or enjoy a good book. Write and reflect in your gratitude journal or stretch and meditate. Really, do whatever brings you joy! Then, climb into bed feeling prepared for the next day so when that alarm goes off, you are ready to hop in the shower and walk out the door!

The benefits of a morning (or evening) routine are numerous:

- ★ A strong morning routine gives you meaningful results that propel you forward and motivate you for the rest of your day
- ★ A set of actions to perform before you start the main events of your day, like making your bed, accomplishes one task done and encourages another
- ★ A deliberate set of activities helps set the focus for the day, removes burnout, and sets you up for success
- ★ Routines are tasks you do deliberately to bring order to your day on a daily basis
- ★ Routines put our brain on autopilot. Once you start, your body will just get up and settle into this new routine

It's important to continuously tailor your routine so that it is always just the right fit for you. If something isn't quite working during this time frame, change it up! Nothing is ever set in stone. Here are a few ideas that you could add to make yours unique to you.

- ★ Exercise - even a 10 minute walk has amazing benefits
- ★ Drink a full glass of water
- ★ Roll out on a foam roller to increase blood flow and range of motion

★ Take a cold shower - Tony Robbins adds this to his morning routine daily - I am not quite there yet!

★ Read a good book

★ Listen to an uplifting podcast

★ Learn something new

★ Pray or meditate

★ Do an act of kindness

★ Make your bed

## Action Step:

1. This week, give it a whirl and see if any combination of this works for you! This is something I have done for years now, and I won't ever go back. I love my time in the morning. It sets the tone for my WHOLE day. Give it a shot if even for one week. It WILL change your life for the better.

## Reflect!

My Morning (or evening) Routine for this week looks like:

Wake up or Begin Evening Routine at _____ (time).

I would like to spend my time doing:

1. _____

2. _____

3. _____

4. _____

5. _____

Now Reflect again! (One week later)

How did it go? What I would change for next week?

_____

_____

_____

_____

_____

_____

_____

_____

_____

_____

_____

_____

_____

_____

_____

_____

_____

_____

*"You will never find time for anything.
If you want time
you must make it."*

*— Charles Buxton*

The next 3 chapters outline 3 BIG strategies that will help you find more time at home to be the most effective, efficient version of yourself.

# Chapter 5: Minutes of Margin and Power Hours

As the lists get longer, the days seem to get shorter. My anxiety goes up, the feeling of being overwhelmed sets in, and all I really want is to be present with my family. I want to ignore all of the "adult tasks" and hang with my kids, watch a movie with my family, or just do nothing at all. But all of the bill paying, grocery shopping, lesson planning, and paper correcting have to get done, and I have to fit it all in somehow!

I bet I am not the only one...

This is where I remember that I need to fall back on minutes of margin in my life and rely on power hours to get the job done while still soaking up quality time with my family.

Building in minutes of margin creates a space where you can do BOTH. Get your work done AND get your family time in. We don't have the luxury of MORE minutes in the day, but we do have a choice with how we use those minutes. Here's where power hours come in!

Are you READY?

Power hours are times during the day when everyone in your family is doing something else. It could be midday when kids are napping and your husband is at work. It could be hours in the late evening or into the night when everyone is in bed. Maybe it's an hour before you normally get up while everyone is still sleeping and the house is quiet. Power hours are pockets of time where you can work uninterrupted and with focus to get things done.

I do mine in the morning. I am an early riser. I function best in the morning, so it makes sense for me to wake up an hour early and get work done. Here is what a typical power hour looks like for me.

> *During the school year I get up at 4:30. Some mornings I hit the treadmill and get a 30 minute run in while listening to an inspiring podcast. Then, I make a cup of coffee, stretch, open my bible, and make my list for the day before ever hopping in the shower.*

> *Other days I wake up, make a cup of coffee (always coffee) and do a few other various things that might include grading papers, paying bills, reading my Bible, or checking and responding to email. Basically I just do things I like or that need to get done AND take me away from the time I want to spend with my family.*

By taking the time to get up and work a power hour, I create time that I can focus on being present with my family. Things that need to get done are getting done, and I am getting the time I crave with the ones I love. WIN, WIN!

The one thing I always do (besides coffee) is make my list for the day before I hop into the shower.

My list helps me begin the day focused and stay that way throughout the day. It also "declutters" my mind. I can let go of something in my mind if it is written down on a piece of paper! I set up my evolving list (mentioned in detail in Chapter 3) in order of priority and get things done accordingly. This leaves me with a sense of accomplishment at the end of the day whether I got everything done or not! Most importantly, it removes the guilt and leaves time to be present with the people I am around all day. I can give them my attention without my mind being elsewhere.

# Action Step:

1.  This week, create a POWER HOUR for yourself. Choose the time of day that works best for you and GET. THINGS. DONE. so you can enjoy and be present in YOUR life!

Ultimately that's what's important to me. The years will pass, and I will have more time to myself when the kids are out of the house. Right now, I can create time in the margins if it means I get more quality family time now.

# *Reflect!*

My power hours this week will look like:

Monday: _____

Tuesday: _____

Wednesday: _____

Thursday: _____

Friday: _____

Saturday: _____

Sunday: _____

What I gained from creating this time:

_____

_____

_____

_____

_____

_____

_____

How I felt after creating power hour space in my life:

_____

_____

_____

_____

_____

_____

_____

_____

_____

_____

_____

_____

_____

_____

_____

_____

_____

"*You get what you focus on.
So focus on
what you want.*"

*– unknown*

# Chapter 6: Focus: Your Day in Chunks

Some days, it feels like all of the things I need to do are physically swirling around my head like a cartoon character on the old cartoon *Tom and Jerry*. As I begin to work on one thing, the next thing pops up, or I see something that triggers a reminder of another thing I need to do.

> It goes a little something like this. I need to clean the kitchen, so I begin. Soon, I notice a sock on the floor. Of course I grab it and throw it in the laundry basket and consequently decide to do a load of laundry. While there, I can't help but notice that the dryer hasn't been emptied since Tuesday. SOOO, I haaaave to open it and pull out the clean laundry, which often leads to folding and taking it to one of the kids' rooms. While there, I remember that permission slip I was going to sign for Chase. So I run up and look for it. An hour later, the kitchen is STILL a mess, and (more importantly) what have I even been doing for a whole hour? My list is still as long as it was when I started.

Do you ever find yourself doing this? Would you like to get through your list, but some things take longer than others, which leads down rabbit trails, task switching and longer lists? If so, I can't wait to share this strategy with you.

Live your day in CHUNKS!

Think back to when you were in middle school. You know how you went to first period math class? When you were there, you focused only on math.

Then to second period English. When you were there, you focused only on English. Take this idea and apply it to your life!

Again like I've stated in previous chapters, start your day by making your list in order of priority. But to activate this strategy, allot specific amounts of time to your most important, time-consuming tasks. Then FOCUS for the whole period of time until it is done.

Ignore the dryer bell, leave the sock on the floor and finish what you are doing! Even if you don't accomplish the entire task, you WILL get SO MUCH MORE DONE by keeping your brain focused on the task at hand. By task switching, you will spend more time DECIDING what to do instead of actually doing what needs to get done.

You can do this at work too. In fact, I 1000% recommend it. Make that list IN ORDER OF PRIORITY, set aside a chunk of time, and then focus until it is done or until the time is up!

Now, you may need a little help to keep all of the distractions at bay. But here is where you anticipate anything that might pull you away and PREPARE!

Put on noise-canceling headphones, change your location, wake up earlier, or stay up later. Do WHATEVER you need to do in order to accomplish the task in its entirety. Save the things that can be done in spite of distractions around for later in the day, or move them down on your list.

## Action Step:

1. This week take one task that is hanging over your head, and schedule a block of time for it. Then buckle down, eliminate task switching, and stay focused until your time is up. I promise you will be so impressed with yourself and want to do more!

# *Reflect!*

This week at home:

I will accomplish _____

_____

by setting aside time (when and where) _____

_____

This week at work:

I will accomplish _____

_____

by setting aside time (when and where)

_____

_____

*"Time has a wonderful way of showing us what really matters."*

*—unknown*

# Chapter 7: Thoughts on Timing Yourself

I don't know about you, but I am finding myself spending more time on Facebook, Instagram, Pinterest and doing things that are mind-numbing instead of mind-fulfilling. (Is that even a word?)

I hate that I can take a quick peek at FB and 45 minutes later I am stilllll scrolling! And when I am done, I feel like I've just wasted 45 minutes of my life.

This can happen easily, and there are times when it is appropriate to just let your brain veg out! I get that! But more times than not, I have needed a strategy to keep myself focused on the task at hand, whether it be a chore or just relaxing to read a book. So here's the secret to being intentional with your unintentional time.....TIME YOURSELF.

Yes, you heard me correctly. It's that easy! Set a timer when you hop onto social media (or just look at the clock.) Give yourself 5, 10, 20 minutes, whatever you intentionally want to spend. Then...surf away! Without the guilt. When your time is up, STOP. It's that easy! (Really!)

The same goes for your intentional time. SET. THAT. TIMER. Read a good book, take a bath, or clean the house. Give yourself an hour and get it done. When the timer goes off, you can move to the next thing.

It is so weird. I don't spend the whole day timing myself, but if I really want to make myself focus, I will set the timer for a desired amount of time and get it done or take time away to relax and rejuvenate, guilt free!

# Action Step:

This week when you sit down to veg out on social media, look at the clock. Set an amount of time to let yourself scroll, and then ENJOY! Just remember to stop when your time is up!

# *Reflect!*

Two areas where I would like to commit to using my time better are:

Area 1: _____ Area 2: _____

Area 1: _____

_____

Amount of time given: _____

_____

How it went! _____

_____

Area 2: _____

_____

Amount of time given: _____

_____

How it went! _____

_____

_____

_____

*"A goal without a plan is just a wish."*

—Antoine de Saint-Exupéry

# Chapter 8: Planning for Ultimate Meal Prep

I have come to the realization that after thousands of trips to the store and hours staring at my family asking them what they want for dinners this week, I LOATHE meal planning and grocery shopping. (Yes, LOATHE)

Seriously, something had to give.

I am just to a point where I am not willing to give up Friday night (or worse yet, Sunday afternoon) figuring out my shopping list for the next week. But, I am also not willing to spend the money going out every night or serving less healthy meals because I am not planning. So.....drum roll please..... here's what I've come up with!

Meal plan for the MONTH! (And every month thereafter... forever... and ever.)

Here's how:

1. Fill out ONE Monthly Meal Calendar for the month. Choose 4 or 5 weeks and write down 4 of your family's favorite meals per week. I only use the meal planner for dinners. They are where I struggle the most. You can do it that way, or do all three meals for each day.

YOU already know what meals your family loves to eat. Just start writing them down. Then if you need a couple more, search Pinterest or check out the TRIED-AND-TRUE recipes that I have on my website www.thisorganizedteacherlife.com! They work well for my picky family!

By choosing 4 meals per week, you will most likely have one night of no cooking (jackpot!) as you clean up the leftovers and give yourself a clean fridge by the end of the week! LOVE, LOVE, LOVE!

*Brainstorm* your *family's favorite meals* here!

_____   _____

_____   _____

_____   _____

_____   _____

_____   _____

_____   _____

_____   _____

_____   _____

_____   _____

_____   _____

_____   _____

_____   _____

_____   _____

# Monthly Meal Calendar

| | Sunday | Monday | Tuesday | Wednesday | Thursday | Friday | Saturday |
|---|---|---|---|---|---|---|---|
| Week 1 | | | | | | | |
| Week 2 | | | | | | | |
| Week 3 | | | | | | | |
| Week 4 | | | | | | | |
| Week 5 | | | | | | | |

2. After naming all of your meals on the Monthly Meal Calendar, add your meals to the Weekly Meal Calendar for each corresponding week (1 week, 1 page), along with the ingredients you will need to add to your shopping list for those particular recipes. Find your FREE Weekly Meal Calendar on my website www.thisorganizedteacherlife.com under RESOURCES.

3. Tuck the actual recipes behind each Weekly Meal Calendar for the week you will be cooking them so you don't waste time looking for them later.

4. Now, group all of your Meal Calendars together starting with the Monthly Calendar on top, and then following with each Weekly Calendar in order (weeks 1-4) with recipes included behind each particular week, stick them in a place that is convenient and easy to access. When it's time for this week's grocery shopping, you'll have the list ready!

5. Finally, when you arrive at the week you want to shop for, either cross off items you already have, OR add your needed items to a list in your phone and head out the door. Better yet, order it online and pick it up! (I use Fred Meyer, but you can use Walmart or whatever is most convenient in your area)

The goal here is to use the SAME CALENDAR every month! No reinventing the wheel. After 4 weeks of your family's faves, start back at week one. If you don't like how it's working, change it up! Add or remove a meal or two, assign meals to different family members, or add your kids into the mix by cooking with them. Just tailor it to meet your family's needs!

Again, you can access all of my meal calendars and our family's TRIED-AND-TRUE recipes for FREE on my website www.thisorganizedteacherlife.com under RESOURCES.

## Action Steps:

1. Go to www.thisorganizedteacherlife.com and click RESOURCES.
2. Print the meal calendars.
3. Get started filling out that monthly calendar first! It's fun to think of all of the recipes your family loves, and it will get you rolling into that next step of the weekly menu. Remember! Once you do this, you are done thinking about it forever!! (You may even want to laminate your lists and recipes to protect from spills and use over time.) Whatever you do, DON'T WAIT my friends!

# Reflect!

I am going to use the meal planner system to make meal planning a breeze. I plan to get started by... _____

_____

_____

_____

_____

_____

_____

_____

_____

_____

_____

_____

_____

_____

_____

_____

_____

_____

_____

_____

# Meal Planner Week 1

| Day | Meal | Shopping List |
| --- | --- | --- |
| Monday | | |
| Tuesday | | |
| Wednesday | | |
| Thursday | | |
| Friday | | |
| Saturday | | |
| Sunday | | |

# Part 2:

## When Your Classroom Works for You

*"The secret of change
is to focus all of your energy,
not on fighting the old,
but on building the new."*

— Socrates

# Chapter 9: Why Back to School is Not About You

Welcome back to school!

And...whether you are a first year teacher or been at it for 20+ years, your back to school may begin in August like mine with recurring nightmares of students screaming down the hallways and climbing up the walls of your classroom.

Or...

Maybe it's like fall of 2020 with the question," How am I going to do all of this... virtually or social-distanced or BOTH?" The students come with problems you can't possibly solve and behavior that has you stumped! The panic and anxiety are so real you already feel like a failure, and YOUR new school year hasn't even begun.

I still, after years of teaching, spend time thinking about my new bunch of kids and wondering how the dynamic will flow.

Will they like me?

Will they respect me?

Will I be able to do a good ENOUGH job?

And then it hit me one day after listening to words from Angela Watson's Truth for Teachers Podcast. The TRUTH is......it's not about ME!

WHAAAAT?

Yep! It's REALLY not! In the world of education, it is said ALL THE TIME. "It's about the KIDS!" We SAY IT and SAY IT and SAY IT, but what does it really mean?

Well, I am learning that it looks a lot like this.

In ANY profession, we can easily make it about ourselves. And when we do, we get anxious and feel inadequate wondering if we will measure up. When presenting, teaching, meeting new patients, or clients, it's easy to second guess if we are the best, most qualified person for the job.

BUT... if you step back and take a look at the people we are

presenting TO,

teaching TO,

speaking TO,

and focus on THEIR needs and how we are going to meet them, the perspective changes.

This year on the first day of school, my focus became LEARNING about my kids from day 1.

>>> Greet each of them EVERY morning.

>>> ASK questions to learn more about the people they are.

>>> THEN and only then, strive to meet their needs.

Make a plan for each student and take steps in succession and get the job done.

It's not about you and your feelings of inadequacy. The perspective has to shift to the person you are serving. All of your anxiety melts away when you are no longer worried about yourself and are focused on others. Then as an added bonus in the world of teaching, the negative behaviors begin to subside or diminish and trust begins to build.

Relationships begin to grow and learning takes place. The cool thing is that this can happen anywhere and in any career. Take an interest in others, let them know that you are listening and take the pressure off of yourself while building relationships. It will pay dividends because... isn't this where your focus should be anyway?

Start here and NOW!

Don't waste another moment!

Especially in years like 2020 when everything is turned on its head.

- ★ Scale back and focus on what is necessary.
- ★ Don't overcomplicate things. (Less is MORE)
- ★ Keep systems simple and consistent.

What your students need now, more than anything, is YOU! So be there and be present.

## Action Steps:

1. Greet your kids by name as they enter your classroom or Zoom meeting every time.
2. Ask attendance questions and take the class time to let them answer. Listen and get to know them.
3. Pick 2 students each class period (keep track of who you've chosen in a checklist) and spend a couple of minutes engaging with them in a genuine way. You will be amazed at how this changes your classroom environment and curbs unwanted behaviors.

# *Reflect!*

What will you do TODAY to shift the perspective from your agenda to "HOW will I SERVE my students?" _____

_____

_____

_____

_____

_____

_____

_____

_____

_____

_____

_____

_____

_____

_____

_____

_____

_____

_____

_____

_____

_____

*"All we have to decide
is what to do with the time
that is given us."*

*-J. R. R Tolken*

# Chapter 10: Creating Boundaries Around Your Time

How were you supposed to know that when you became a teacher your home and work lives would become one with give and take playing tug-o-war at the center?

It all started with just a few more minutes here and there that eventually turned into hours answering that "quick" email at 7:30 pm, or cutting out that laminating in front of the TV while having "quality time" with your family.

We are so committed to doing the best job for our kids at school. We come early, stay late, work on weekends, and work in the evening. We are continuously giving "just a little more time" to school or bringing work home so that it can seep into our home lives.

Right now, boundaries around our time as teachers are more necessary than ever. If you live in the grey area not only with yourself, but with parents and students, you are inviting work to bleed into your personal life until your personal life becomes non-existent!

If you begin the school year by answering emails and phone calls at all hours of the day and night, parents and students will expect you to respond to them at all hours. You are teaching them how to treat your time. And if you allow it at first, you are training them not to see and respect your time at home as separate from your work at school. So keep this work life/home life separate. You need to set boundaries!

Here's how!

★ From the beginning of the year, set up "office hours" with your parents. For example, "I will be answering voicemails and emails from 8am until 4pm Monday through Friday. If you leave me a message after 4pm, I will get back to you on the following work day during those hours."

★ Post this in your back to school letters, on your website, and at open house! Then, STICK TO IT! This may be the hardest part. But make a pledge to yourself to stick to it for a month. Work hard to build that routine and create a habit. The more consistent you are, the better it will work.

★ Use your time at school wisely. Do the most important things. Make your list (in order of priority). If things don't get done, move it to tomorrow's list or maybe take it off all together.

★ Really try to avoid taking work home at all costs. Grade during your prep time, create a set planning time before or after school each week, and commit time at home for family time.

# Action Steps:

1. Determine your office hours. Add them to your website, your open house information, and send them in an email to your parents.

2. Make a pledge to yourself that you will keep these hours and only respond during those times.

3. Turn school off when you are at home. Be present with the ones you love and enjoy time with them.

# *Reflect!*

I will add boundaries to my life by _____

_____

_____

_____

_____

_____

_____

_____

_____

_____

_____

_____

_____

_____

_____

_____

_____

_____

*"Start by doing what's necessary;*
*then do what's possible;*
*then suddenly you are doing the impossible."*

*– St. Francis of Assisi*

# Chapter 11: Conquering Being Overwhelmed: Learn to Plan Your Day to be the Most Productive Version of Yourself

Let's be honest, our days are PACKED! We are up to our eyeballs in schedules, homework, running kids from practice to practice, food prep, laundry, etc, etc, etc.

What do we do when we are in a constant state of being overwhelmed? We complain, we get frustrated, and we vent! Our homes become tense, the relationships we value most are put on the back burner, and we either crumble OR "grizzly bear" on through with no thought to who we run over. And rightfully so. Right?

[Wrong]

Who actually likes to live in this place? I know I don't.

Well here are a few thoughts on this that might help the situation and shift perspective.

- ★ PLAN
- ★ BE PRESENT (at work and at home)
- ★ MAKE TIME FOR FUN
- ★ COMMIT

A teacher's day consists of limited time before and after school, a prep period and a 30 minute lunch without students. The rest of the day is spent teaching kids.

The thing is, your time is GOLDEN! It is finite. You cannot add hours to the day, so MAKE THE MOST of what you have and GET. STUFF. DONE!

Map out your time and use it allll! BE the most productive you can be during your work hours, so that when those hours are over, you can be present at home with the ones you love.

Here's a little how to:

[Before school]

- ★  Before you jump into the day, PLAN for what you want to get done.
- ★  Make that list and put it in order of priority! Then, move through it!
- ★  When you physically get to work, get started! Jump right in with those most important things first. I know that when I stop to chat, I burn through time. So DON'T!
- ★  Set aside time to visit with colleagues (maybe lunch) and stick to it!
- ★  Advertise that you are going to try to use your time more wisely at school, so that your coworkers understand that coming in to visit for 30 minutes is not going to help you (or them) get things done!

[Big projects]

- ★  When you are working on those big ticket projects like goal setting or scheduling or planning for that big unit, make sure that every day you take ONE step toward the completion of that goal. Name the ONE THING you can do TODAY to get closer to completing that goal and do it! Before you know it, it's DONE!

[Prep time]

★ Grade, grade, grade!!! Close your door and turn on some soft music and grade like CRAZY. Don't spend time running up and down the hall to copy. Grading is my nemesis! And I hate to bring it home! So I use EVERY. SPARE. MINUTE. (when not with students) at school getting that grading DONE!

[After school]

★ When the kids are out the door for the day, DON'T SIT DOWN. Move around your classroom to get ALL THE THINGS ready for tomorrow. If I sit down initially, I fall into the email surfing trap, and I don't get up because (to be honest) I am TIRED! But those other things around my room still need to get done! So do them FIRST, then move to your desk, finish grading, plan, and last (before you head out the door) answer emails. Give yourself a finite amount of time to do that, so you don't spend time lingering. If an email is going to take too much time, set up an appointment to call that person and discuss the situation!

Now head home!

Engage with your family! Talk in the car, cook and eat together, walk the dog, take an exercise class, or find something you all like to watch and just hang out!

PLAN for that time and CONNECT with those you love or refresh and recharge. THIS is the most valuable time of your day. Work is going to be there in the morning. And you will be more productive at work if you take care of yourself and your family outside of work!

## Action Step:

1. Pick ONE! Choose one strategy from this chapter and implement it this week!

# *Reflect!*

This week I will try (strategy) by _____

_____

_____

_____

_____

_____

_____

_____

_____

_____

_____

_____

_____

_____

_____

_____

_____

_____

_____

_____

_____

_____

*"Relationships before Rigor*
*Grace before Grades*
*Patience before Programs*
*Love before Lessons"*

*-Dr. Brad Johnson*

# Chapter 12: 5 Brilliant Ways to Make Grading a Breeze

As teachers, we spend HOURS grading every week in addition to the ongoing feedback we give our students all throughout the day as they work on assignments during class time.

I finally came to a point in my teaching career where I was fed up and bogged down with the amount of papers that needed to be graded and found myself grading just to grade. I made sure that if I gave an assignment, it was graded, and that that number landed exactly where it needed to be in the grade book. I was taught to grade everything I assigned to students. I always thought, why assign it if it's not being graded? How is that worth it to my students? But as I moved along in my teaching career, I learned that I could not go at this pace forever. I was burning out. There had to be a way to create balance, and I needed to find a way to grade what they needed to know and give meaningful feedback that didn't take all night, every night.

First and foremost, the why. WHY are we grading in the first place?

Contrary to what I initially thought, grading is not just to put a percentage in the grade book. It's not to "catch" students not doing the job.

The REASON we grade is to give our students FEEDBACK and to ultimately GUIDE our teaching. Our students need to know where they are in relation to meeting the standard we are teaching, and by grading, we can do this.

My greatest bit of advice when it comes to grading is this, GRADE IN A TIMELY MANNER OR AS QUICKLY AS POSSIBLE! By doing this, the information you are getting is fresh and meaningful to you and your students and can be used for immediate feedback.

**News Flash!** You don't have to grade everything! Some assignments are meant solely for practice. It is rare that your students will have mastered the standard after the first lesson. Make sure you teach and practice, then grade for an accurate measure of your students' success toward the goal.

Now to the strategies that have CHANGED MY LIFE when it comes to grading...

1.  BEFORE YOU EVEN START, always have a class list check off. This is my staple! I use one list TWICE for EVERY assignment. Here are some of the templates I use. They are available for you for FREE on my website www.thisorganizedteacherlife.com under the RESOURCES tab.

| Assignment __MATH__ | | |
|---|---|---|
| Name | Turned In | Grade |
| | | |
| | | |
| | | |
| | | |
| | | |
| | | |
| | | |
| | | |
| | | |
| | | |
| | | |
| | | |
| | | |
| | | |
| | | |
| | | |
| | | |
| | | |
| | | |
| | | |
| | | |
| | | |

| Assignment __READING__ | | |
|---|---|---|
| Name | Turned In | Grade |
| | | |
| | | |
| | | |
| | | |
| | | |
| | | |
| | | |
| | | |
| | | |
| | | |
| | | |
| | | |
| | | |
| | | |
| | | |
| | | |
| | | |
| | | |
| | | |
| | | |

| Assignment __WRITING__ | | |
|---|---|---|
| Name | Turned In | Grade |
| | | |
| | | |
| | | |
| | | |
| | | |
| | | |
| | | |
| | | |
| | | |
| | | |
| | | |
| | | |
| | | |
| | | |
| | | |
| | | |
| | | |
| | | |
| | | |

assignment tracker

| | MON | 4-27 | TUES | 4-28 | WED | 4-29 | THURS | 4-30 | FRI | 5-1 |
|---|---|---|---|---|---|---|---|---|---|---|
| Student Name | Reading | Math | Reading | Math | Reading | Math | Reading | Math | Reading | Math |
| | | | | | | | | | | |
| | | | | | | | | | | |
| | | | | | | | | | | |
| | | | | | | | | | | |
| | | | | | | | | | | |
| | | | | | | | | | | |
| | | | | | | | | | | |
| | | | | | | | | | | |
| | | | | | | | | | | |
| | | | | | | | | | | |
| | | | | | | | | | | |
| | | | | | | | | | | |
| | | | | | | | | | | |
| | | | | | | | | | | |
| | | | | | | | | | | |
| | | | | | | | | | | |
| | | | | | | | | | | |

Assignment _____

| | Name | Turned in / Grade | |
|---|---|---|---|
| 1 | | | |
| 2 | | | |
| 3 | | | |
| 4 | | | |
| 5 | | | |
| 6 | | | |
| 7 | | | |
| 8 | | | |
| 9 | | | |
| 10 | | | |
| 11 | | | |
| 12 | | | |
| 13 | | | |
| 14 | | | |
| 15 | | | |
| 16 | | | |
| 17 | | | |
| 18 | | | |
| 19 | | | |
| 20 | | | |
| 21 | | | |
| 22 | | | |
| 23 | | | |
| 24 | | | |
| 25 | | | |
| 26 | | | |
| 27 | | | |

Assignment _____

| | Name | Turned in / Grade | |
|---|---|---|---|
| 1 | | | |
| 2 | | | |
| 3 | | | |
| 4 | | | |
| 5 | | | |
| 6 | | | |
| 7 | | | |
| 8 | | | |
| 9 | | | |
| 10 | | | |
| 11 | | | |
| 12 | | | |
| 13 | | | |
| 14 | | | |
| 15 | | | |
| 16 | | | |
| 17 | | | |
| 18 | | | |
| 19 | | | |
| 20 | | | |
| 21 | | | |
| 22 | | | |
| 23 | | | |
| 24 | | | |
| 25 | | | |
| 26 | | | |
| 27 | | | |

To use the grading templates, number your students alphabetically, then check off work once it is turned in. (Or better yet, have your students do it if they are in-person.) Then, I record the actual grade after it is corrected. The class list checkoff is attached to the top of the stack of in-person papers and keeps them in order so that by glancing at the stack, I know who is missing the assignment and can quickly enter grades in the grade book when ready.

From here, I use different techniques for each subject.

1. When teaching math, I grade as soon as the papers come in while students are still working independently. I check quickly and call kids back to pick up their paper and fix mistakes. This way, my students know if they have the concept before the class period has ended. If they need help, they ask then, and I know if I need to re-teach or move on. This works virtually as well. Make them pop on the meet and let you know that it is turned in. Look over it quickly, tell them which ones need fixing, and ask if they need help. This is a great way to get an instant "pulse" on each student.

2. For writing, I always use a rubric! I make sure that I have taught to the rubric first, which makes it SUPER EASY to grade. It doesn't need to be fancy. Just add what NEEDS to be included for this specific piece of writing and give it point values. You ONLY grade what is on that rubric.

Google Classroom trick: You can add a rubric you have already used or create a new one and add it directly to your Google Assignment, so your virtual students have it available as they are working.

1. For all other in-person assignments, make sure you have a WORK TURN IN box. From day one, teach your students where to turn in work, so it is never a mystery. Then, one of my classroom jobs is to have a STUDENT put the papers in number order, check off who has turned them in, using the class checkoff list, and attach the list to the top of the stack for me. I know immediately by look-

ing at the list attached to the top of the pile which students are done and can remind the students who are not just by glancing at the stack.

2. And like I've said before, **grade papers during your prep period!** Shut your door, turn on some soft music and get to work. It always takes time to get started, but once you get going, it goes fast. If someone stops in to ask a question, you can pick up again right away after they leave.

Also, remember, not EVERYTHING needs to go in that grade book! Make sure that what you put in the grade book is an accurate measure of your student's success toward the standard you are teaching. Check in with your district to make sure you are adhering to their standards, but a good rule of thumb is two graded entries per week, per subject.

# Action Step:

1. Pick one! Choose one grading strategy that you are not currently using, and implement it for one week. Tweak and modify as necessary, but take this initial step to begin to take control of your grading.

This week, I will try _____

_____

_____

_____

_____

_____

_____

# Reflect!

How'd it go?

After one week circle back and reflect on how well it worked, what you would change, and what you want to try next! _____

_____

_____

_____

_____

_____

_____

_____

_____

_____

_____

_____

_____

_____

_____

_____

_____

*"It's not the load that breaks you down, it's the way you carry it."*

*– unknown*

# Chapter 13: Brain Breaks to Increase Energy and Productivity

Do you find yourself wanting to be MORE PRODUCTIVE and feel more ENERGY? You start out fresh and ready to go, but after an hour, are you ready for a nap? Do you want to squeeze the most from each day by being your best self and by putting your best foot forward?

What if I told you that **brain breaks** are your answer?

Brain breaks are usually thought of for kids. We see teachers adding them throughout the day as movement breaks to get students up and moving. However, these quick breaks away from the task at hand are immensely important for adults as well. Research shows that a quick 2-3 minute break every 60 minutes releases stress and increases energy and productivity.

Even if you love the work you do, you may find yourself getting tired and trying to push through tasks thinking that you are going to get more done if you just keep going. The truth is, by sticking with the task for longer than an hour, you become LESS PRODUCTIVE and your energy fades. Pushing through increases stress and contributes to poor posture. So let's do better! Here's how!

**Every 60 minutes** throughout your work day, set a timer (if you need to) and GET UP! Take a quick walk around your workplace, grab a quick drink of water and sit back down, take 4 or 5 deep breaths and set your mind on the task ahead. Visualize what you want to get done. Then, focus and be productive. AVOID email. This is your time to CHECK OUT and refresh!

You may not do it every hour at first, but aim for 3 times a day and work into it. I promise you will feel less stress and more rejuvenated and able to conquer all the tasks! The difference will be your energy level. Want more energy? Do this! You will feel happier too!

# Release

I also use a deep breathing technique that was inspired by author and speaker Brendon Burchard's Release Meditation Technique (Burchard, 2014) when needing a break or transitioning into new parts of my day. It goes a little something like this...

When you are taking a quick brain break, take time to stop and breathe. Take 4 slow, deep breaths breathing in through your nose and out through your mouth. Close your eyes and as you breathe out, repeat the word *release*. It is amazing how just repeating that word makes your shoulders drop and your stress level decrease.

I do this just before I get out of my car before heading into work in the morning or when standing next to the microwave waiting for my lunch to heat. It also works well after you have pulled into the driveway and get ready to head into the house for the evening. This technique helps you leave work at work and open your mind to be completely focused and present at home. You will be surprised at how well this works.

**In the Classroom:** Schedule brain breaks for you and your kids alike! I have them written in my daily schedule on the board. (so the kids hold me accountable) If we aren't moving every hour, I schedule movement and meditation. Our FAVORITE is www.gonoodle.com! We do something active and then we do a FLOW meditation to get focused again!

Sometimes we just do jumping jacks, hop on one foot and then the other, or do lunges around the room. Other times we stretch and focus on different muscles. One of my favorite focus activities is teaching them how to listen. We close our eyes for a full 30 seconds and listen hard to whatever we can hear. It's amazing to discover what is going on around you if you just stop to listen. Check out my website www.thisorganizedteacherlife. com for more brain break ideas.

## Action Step:

Today, build in 3 short brain breaks. Write the times down and actually stop what you are doing and move your body for 2-3 minutes and take 4 deep breaths. Watch your stress melt away and your focus and energy increase!

# Reflect!

Today I will build in 3 short brain breaks at these times: _____, _____, _____.

This is how I felt after taking those short breaks. _____

_____

_____

_____

_____

_____

_____

_____

_____

"*Good order
is the foundation
of all things.*"

–Edmund Burke

# Chapter 14: A Place For Everything: Organizing that Never-Ending Paperwork at Home and at School

As a teacher the paperwork is NEVER-ENDING!

And how do you keep track of it all so that you have the option to come back to it AND actually finish it?

How do you keep student work separate from teacher work and notes home or to-do's separate from those staff meeting notes?

How do you keep it all from piling up on your desk far from done and leaving you in a state of despair by the end of the day?

Here is how I have managed to keep my sanity and stay on top of the paper game.

**2 IN-boxes!** (In the classroom. For HOME keep reading...)

The first IN-box is for papers that I need to deal with directly. Notes home, lunch money, permission slips, etc. This is on my desk, and the kids know exactly where it is and what it is used for. This keeps them from handing me notes in the morning or at any time during the day. It also keeps them from setting notes on my desk and me from losing them in the deep abyss that is my desk during the day.

The next basket is in another location, but still remains remotely close to my desk so that I don't have to travel across the room to get to it. It contains all turned in student work. Throughout the day, kids turn in work from all class periods. Another student, (class job - grading helper) organizes the pile multiple times during the day using a class list designed specifically for this purpose. This way all of the piles are paper clipped according to assignment and organized in alphabetical order so I know exactly who has turned them in and who is missing the assignment. When I am ready to grade, the papers are labeled and ready to go. Find the FREE editable grading checklist template I use on my website www.thisorganizedteacherlife.com under Resources.

The SECRET to managing ALL the paper is to have a place for it! This goes for the classroom as well as at home! It's frustrating to have papers all over your desk and similarly all over the house.

The IN-box is your starting place at HOME. It contains the papers until you can get to them. Place a basket in a convenient place and add all of the mail, notes home from school, bills - virtually everything that comes into the house weekly.

Here's where the magic happens!

Now, pick a time during the week to go through these papers. Maybe Sunday afternoon for example. Sit down, shred the junk mail, sign the papers from school, pay those bills, whatever it takes to get through the stack. But whatever you do, make sure that basket is empty when you get done! Make sure you are accomplishing the task at hand or moving the paper to another location for storage. For example, the Explanation of Benefits from your last dental appointment needs to be filed in a space labeled EOB's.

There is something freeing about having a place for every piece of paper. Your paper should be either thrown away, shredded if you don't need it, or filed where you can find it if you do!

## Action Steps:

1.  Remember! Baby steps! Start with the IN-box. Then as you move through the pile and come up with papers that need a home, start a new file. Move that shredder to a place that is close and convenient (ours is in the garage right next to the door, so some junk mail doesn't even make it into the house).

2.  Start today! By doing this you are on a real track to freedom from paper!

# *Reflect!*

My IN-boxes for school will go _____ and _____

I will go through the first one at (day(s) of the week and time)

_____

I will go through the second one at (day(s) of the week and time)

_____

My IN-box for home will go _____

I will go through this IN-box every week at (day and time) _____

_____

"*One of the greatest gifts you can give to anyone is the gift of your attention.*"

*–unknown*

# Chapter 15: Taking Your Parent-Teacher Conferences from Mundane to Magnificent

Have you ever wondered how to take your parent-teacher conferences to the next level?

Do you prepare and then hold your breath hoping for no surprises?

Do you let the meetings run themselves and react to whatever happens when it happens?

THAT is how I ran my parent-teacher conferences for years. I prepared and presented and hoped for the best. For the most part, that worked for me until I had that one parent who came with information that was totally unexpected. "Johnny hates school. Paul has been bullying him on the playground for the last two months, and you aren't doing anything about it."

OR

How about a situation where for whatever reason you don't have a good relationship with a parent and haven't ever worked well together. One that you can't seem to please. I don't know about you, but those conferences are ones that I dread and do not look forward to. They make me unbelievably uncomfortable.

But, as adults and for the sake of the student, we all need to figure out how to make these meetings productive and meaningful.

So, let's dive in!

Here's how:

First, VISUALIZE that meeting, conference, or even that lesson or inter-action with a colleague. What do you expect it to look like? How has it gone before?

Next, PREPARE. Get to KNOW the people that you are going to be inter-acting with. What are they like? Do they always respond a certain way? Are they quick to judge? Are they quick to take things in a direction that is not productive?

Now, IMAGINE how they will respond to topics that will be covered, and IMAGINE how YOU can respond to take the discussion back to being productive again. Research and prepare yourself for the typical response you might get from this person. Have a few responses of your own ready to go. What words will you use? See the entire thing play out in your mind. This is a technique you can use in so many situations. This is not just for conferences.

Then, PRACTICE. Practice different scenarios and SAY THE WORDS you will use to respond. The more comfortable you get saying those words, the easier they will come out of your mouth when you need them.

Instead of waiting for life to come at you, prepare, direct and guide inter-actions to create the best possible outcome for everyone involved. Stop thinking of life as happening TO you and start thinking of it happening FOR you! Take part in this story and help write it!

## Action Steps: When preparing for a particularly nerve-wracking conference or meeting...

1.  Visualize problems from the past or potential problems that might arise.

2.  Prepare possible solutions that could help neutralize potential problems.

3.  Imagine a productive conversation.

4.  Practice different words, phrases, and responses to get the conversation back on track and lead to a productive outcome.

Try this with a situation you are working on right now.

Right now, I am preparing for a meeting with _____

_____

Visualize: (How do you think it will go? How has it gone before?)

_____

_____

_____

_____

_____

_____

Prepare: (Get to know the people you are meeting with. What are they like? How do they react or respond?)

_____

_____

_____

_____

_____

_____

_____

Imagine: (Imagine the topics covered. How can you respond to keep the conversation productive and positive? Think of words or phrases you can use.)

_____

_____

_____

_____

_____

_____

Practice: (Practice those scenarios. Actually say the words and practice how you will respond.)

_____

_____

_____

_____

_____

_____

# Reflect!

How did your meeting go after using this strategy?

_____

_____

_____

_____

_____

_____

_____

_____

_____

_____

_____

_____

_____

_____

_____

_____

_____

_____

*"Celebrate what's working.*
*Change what's not."*

*– unknown*

# Chapter 16: Creating Personalized Behavior Expectations With Your Class

I t is so important to establish goals and set expectations at the beginning of every school year. BUT, it is equally important to revisit and reestablish these goals and expectations at any point in the year if you feel that things aren't going as you originally intended. I have created a foolproof method to get student behavior back on track at any point in the school year!

I really like to use this system after Winter Break AND after Spring Break to reengage and keep those expectations high.

Here's how to use it:

First things first! You need to get the kids to BUY-IN! Buy-in is of ULTIMATE importance as we set expectations. The goal here is to create a sense of community in your classroom. This is a place where you (and your students) spend hours a day for the rest of the school year. So what do you and your class want it to look like?

Sit down with your students and MAKE A LIST of behaviors that we all DON'T want to see in our classroom. Behaviors that make it hard to learn. Behaviors that bring us down or make us feel sad or angry. Then list these behaviors AND make a parallel list of equally important consequences to those behaviors. Agreed upon by the majority!

This can be used in our face-to-face classrooms as well as in our virtual learning environments. Students know what behaviors "bug" them, and it is powerful to have discussions like this because students set the standard and their peers notice that and begin to raise the bar for themselves.

From there, MAKE IT OFFICIAL! Put it into an Expectation Contract that can be printed and signed by each individual student and a parent. Grab your FREE editable version at my website www.thisorganizedteacherlife.com under the RESOURCES tab.

Next, COMMUNICATE your contract with parents by sending the contract home with kids. Print one for each student to read and sign, so that they can explain how THEY came to create this document as a class.

Then, POST expectations around the room as a reminder of what everyone committed to. I printed out about six at the elementary level and had the kids hang them around the room. You may only need or want one at the upper grade levels. This way, it's not teachers against students. It's us, creating our own environment where we GET to spend all the hours until June!

Finally, HOLD EACH OTHER ACCOUNTABLE! Teach the kids how to encourage one another if they see them exhibiting any of these behaviors, and talk about how we react when someone holds us accountable. (Help kids to give gentle reminders and point to the expectations if they see someone not holding up their end of the bargain.)

## Action Steps:

1. Hold that class meeting today. Carve out a little bit of time and get the conversation rolling. You will be surprised at how much kids want to be a part of the decision making process to improve the classroom environment.
2. Grab your editable templates at www.thisorganizedteacherlife.com under the RESOURCES tab and create your unique Expec-

tation Contracts and posters to send home and post throughout your classroom.

3. Teach kids to hold each other accountable in a gentle positive way, by pointing to the posters and using words that are encouraging instead of condemning.

# *Reflect* on how you might run your class meeting this week.

This week, I will hold my class meeting on (day) _____ at (time) _____.

I plan to discuss

_____

_____

_____

_____

_____

_____

_____

_____

_____

_____

_____

_____

_____

_____

*"Individually we are a drop.
But together,
we are an ocean."*

*– Ryunosuke Satoro*

# Chapter 17: Building Unity When Kids Are Unraveling

If you have been teaching for any amount of time, you know that as vacation approaches, students have many different reactions to the sunny, relaxed, easygoing days off. Most are excited and can't wait for swimming, playing, and sleeping in, but many are terrified of no schedule, lack of time with a trusted adult, and the dark abyss of endless unknown days consisting of different, unfamiliar people coming in and out of their lives. They are unnerved by not knowing what each day will look like, where they will go and what they will do. As this anxiety plays out, kids become irritable, unkind, and short tempered with one another. The best of friends are arguing, and no one has even an ounce of patience for anyone else.

I don't know about you, but all of this attention to student behavior puts a wrench in me trying to squeeze in the last bit of math curriculum and teach it to mastery before the end of the year (insert sarcasm here).

In an attempt to bring fluidity back to my classroom, I have integrated a couple of different team building activities into our days. I tend to rotate back and forth with these two as they seem to be the kids' favorites. Each one is designed to help kids get to know each other better and teach them how to give compliments about things their peers do well and excel in.

The two activities play out like this:

**Table Topics**: I have the family version that I bought on Amazon and brought into the classroom. It is $25 and comes with 135 questions that are thought provoking but easy for kids of all ages to answer. With 15 minutes left at the end of the day, I pull out a question and read it to the whole class. Everyone gets a minute to think and then when the first few kids come up with an answer, they raise their hands and wait to be called on. This way, if others need more time or a few ideas, they can listen to some of their peers go first. I find that the kids listen intently to one another and truly enjoy hearing unique, personal details about their friends. They get excited about what they have in common and enjoy having more common interests to talk about throughout the day.

**Bucket Filler Cards**: (used at the elementary level, but can be adapted for older kids) These magical cards go along with the story Have you Filled a Bucket Today? By Carol McCloud and David Messing. At the beginning of the year, I read this adorable book. It talks about how you can lift people up with simple acts and loving words all day long. It describes how acts of kindness and caring words work together to lift a spirit and make others feel better about themselves and the world around them.

Next, I give out bucket filler cards. You can make your own with blank 3x5 index cards or find many adorable ones on Teachers Pay Teachers. These cards work a little differently. I have each student take a card first thing in the morning with the name of another student on the back. They always go for a student that they haven't had yet. Eventually they will have the same student twice. Once they have a card, they keep it a secret (they love this) but watch this person intently, looking for good things they do throughout the day. When they notice something, they (again secretly) write it down on the note card. Then at the end of the day (usually the last 15 minutes) we read each one out loud from one student to another highlighting all of the wonderful things they did during the day. The students light up when their personal card is read, and the student reading glows with enjoyment knowing that they are making their peer feel special.

For use at a middle school or even HS level, assign names at the beginning of the week. Give students a time period to have them back. (end of the class period or end of the week) Notes could be left anonymously with the teacher, or put in a jar or specific place when finished for review and then passed out at the beginning of the day the following day. I know a creative teacher that has her students create envelopes with their names on them at the beginning of the year. That way she can just slip a note of encouragement in the envelope and hand it back from time to time.

Every student can benefit from kind words spoken by a peer. This is just one way to brighten a mood or change an attitude. No signatures are needed. These can be absolutely anonymous.

## Action steps:

1. Find a list online or buy a deck of conversation cards that seem appropriate for the grade level you teach.
2. Choose a time, beginning or end of the day or class period that you will be consistent in setting aside this time.
3. Get started! Don't wait! Your kids will absolutely love this and it really does help pull out the kindness that still exists in their hearts!

## *Reflect!*

I plan to use activities like this to build unity in my classroom this week by

_____

_____

_____

_____

_____

_____

_____

"*Small acts,*
*when multiplied by millions of*
*people,*
*can transform the world.*"

–Howard Zinn

# Chapter 18: Mini Challenge: Two Proven Strategies to Lift Your Mood Instantly

[B eing a Gift to a Coworker]

Have you ever thought about how you feel when someone encourages you, sees you, thanks you, or drops you a note of support? I know that it makes me feel appreciated, valued, and loved. It brightens my day and changes my outlook.

How do you feel when you turn the tables and encourage, see, thank, or support someone else? Often, it feels even better, right?

So, how often do you actually show this type of support to someone you see regularly?

What would it look like if we all did this even once a week?

It might look like turning someone's whole day around.

- ★ It might look like more smiles in the hallway.
- ★ It might begin to cultivate more of us doing the exact same thing.

Because... Positivity breeds positivity!

It is hard to ignore the feelings you feel when someone is kind to you. Most often you want to do something kind too. So imagine if many or even most of us started doing something kind for someone else one day a week. Imagine what that would do to the environment we live and work in. Especially right now.

So let's do this! This week surprise a coworker or someone you see regularly!

Here's an easy way to do it!

A simple note. I LOVE beautiful note cards. So recently, I bought a box of these gorgeous little note cards with perfect inspirational quotes in them. Right now I am using ThoughtFulls (locally made in the US). Find them at www.live-inspired.com.

I bring this adorable little box to work, along with a bag of Dove Chocolates. (Any small treat will work.) Then, every morning I try to think of someone to surprise with an encouraging note and a chocolate. It motivates me, and encourages them at the same time.

If you don't have note cards, simply jot down a word of encouragement and slip it on their desk, or even better, give a compliment! It doesn't take a lot of effort to brighten someone's day and give the atmosphere a little boost. Try it!

[How the TONE OF YOUR VOICE can change YOUR mood]

Have you ever thought about how you answer the phone when someone like your significant other, sibling, mom, dad, or just someone constant in your life is calling? My bet is the tone of your voice is flat and you're thinking, "What do they want?"

Am I right?

When you are greeted with a flat voice, how does that make you feel? Do you want to continue that conversation? Most likely not. It makes you feel undervalued and less important. Who wants to be treated like that, ever?

So why can't we change this? Part of feeling happy is choosing to be joyful in every mundane moment and THIS is an easy one!

This week, pick up the phone with a joyful tone in your voice EVERY TIME a person calls. Greet them with the happiness you save for those you are really excited to see or talk to. When they hear your tone, they will most likely reciprocate the happiness.

Imagine the magnitude of this!

How do you think the person on the other end will FEEL when you answer sounding happy to talk to them? How will they then treat you and others when they feel valued by YOU? How will YOU feel when you continuously add joy to your tone? That joy is a constant elevator of your own mood and will lift you up as well! Win! Win!

## Action Steps:

1. Take action this week! Order those amazing note cards and grab a bag of chocolate and take them to work.
2. Start today by answering those mundane phone calls with a happy, joyful tone every time.

## *Reflect!*

This week I will surprise 2 people with a note and a gift. Those 2 people are:

_____

_____

_____

_____

_____

_____

_____

"*Wherever you are,
be all there.*"

–Jim Elliot

# Chapter 19: Don't Stop! 4 Ways to Successfully Bring This School Year to a Close and Jump Start Next Year

I am such a linear thinker. I can't move on until I have accomplished what is in front of me. So when I see my coworkers getting ready for next year before this year is even over, it completely blows my mind and literally makes me panic. I am AMAZED at how they make all the copies, get packets prepared, and are planned for the first couple weeks of school before the kids are even out of the classroom!

Don't get me wrong, I WISH I could be more like this! But here's the thing. I can only focus on One. Thing. At. A. Time. To do it well. And although I know the paperwork is monumental and the more organized you are NOW, the easier it will be in the fall, I KNOW what I need to do right now is keep my focus on the kids currently in my classroom and finish the job I started back in September.

Here's how I end the school year and jump start the new year while maintaining my sanity: (well, for the most part)

### 1. Be Present and Stay Connected

The first thing I do at the end of the year is the same thing I did at the beginning of the school year. I focus on being present when I am in my classroom with students. I still greet my kids at the door in the morning. I do 2 minute check-in's with those tough kids and keep connected with what is going on in their lives.

As a class, we work on culminating projects that involve and put into action all that we have learned throughout the year. We present, we discuss, and we celebrate how we have grown. We talk and have conversations, and we learn from, agree, and disagree with each other. Whatever you do academically, stay connected. This will help with behavior too!

## 2. Break out the Ice Breakers

Pull out the Get-to-Know-You games you did at the beginning of the year! They are so much fun, but in a more unique way now that you know your students and they know each other better. The conversations are deeper and more genuine now at the end of the year. One of my favorites, like I have said before - I love pulling out a Table Topic and giving everyone a chance to share. It spurs on laughter and "me too" conversation that makes kids feel a true sense of belonging up until the very end. If you are looking for ideas, just hop onto Pinterest and search "get to know you games for students." You will find plenty to choose from there.

## 3. Begin Thinking About Next Year

I struggle with this because, you know, one thing at a time. But here are a couple of ways to get started so that you won't have mounds of work to do once the kids are gone.

**Classroom set up!**

**First: WALLS**

Look around your room starting with your walls.

TARGETS: Are your learning targets and goals in a prominent place where you can easily access them and your students know where to locate them at a moment's notice? It's important they know the "why" of what is being taught.

ANCHOR CHARTS: Do you have a space for anchor charts digital or otherwise that can be removed and/or added to daily? These are places that kids will refer back to when working, so make them easy for you to use and easy for students to see.

STUDENT WORK: How will you highlight your student's work? This year, I want to make this a MUCH LARGER part of my classroom. I want the focus to be less on showcasing learning targets and more on accentuating anchor charts made WITH students and celebrating actual student work. I have gotten so many unique ideas for new ways to do this from creative teachers on Pinterest and Instagram.

Sketch out how you want your walls to look when you come back in the fall, create signs and posters, and laminate them now (not when EVERYONE is back in the fall and the laminator is running 24/7).

**Next: FURNITURE AND LEARNING SPACE**

MAIN TEACHING SPACE AND GATHERING AREA: Start with a common area where you would like to have kids gather on the floor or in alternative seating. Even older kids don't mind gathering on the floor from time to time to change it up. You will most likely want this near your main teaching space. Once you have designated this, move on to where to place your desk.

TEACHER DESK, WORK TURN-IN, FILES: Place your desk away from the main flow of the classroom. Make sure work turn-in, files, and things that you need when at your desk are within a few steps from it so that you aren't crossing the room 16 times every time you sit down to work.

STUDENT DESKS: The only rule of thumb here is that you have space for everyone to flow through the room. There are so many ideas on Pinterest. Just pick one you like and go with it!

**Now: BRAIN DUMP!**

Academically and socially, make a 2 column list of what worked well and what did not. Let that list drive your thinking, learning, and work over the summer. For instance, my summer work this year will focus on learning how to plan digitally, how to integrate more non-fiction analyzing and writing, and taking my students' reading fluency and comprehension to the next level.

What do you want to enhance, change, or work on for next year? Choose a few of those items from your list and commit to making change in these areas over the summer. Do some research or take a class, but commit to doing this better next year. Don't take on too much! Make it manageable so that you can accomplish it and do it well!

What *Worked* Well This Year | What *Did Not Work* Well This Year

#### 4. Take Time to NOT Think About School

I like to take the first part of summer and focus on my family and myself. I have fun, I work on home projects, I read (for fun), I run, and I rest. I usually give myself a deadline date (usually August 1) and put school aside until then. I find that if I do this, I can't wait to jump back in and I work with excitement and diligence when it is time.

I hope this helps you get through the last few weeks and finish the school year STRONG so that you can walk away for the summer, rest, regroup, and come back refreshed and prepared to start again in the fall.

## Action Steps:

1. Be present with students at school during the last few weeks. Engage, play icebreaker games, and plan big culminating projects where kids can present and discuss.

2. Before you leave for the summer sketch out the layout of your room and set goals for summer and the first few weeks of school.

3. Take time during the summer to completely disengage from school. Rest and recharge so that you are excited to come back when it's time!

## *Reflect!*

My end of the year plans are to _____

_____

_____

_____

_____

_____

# Part 3:

## When Self Care Becomes a Priority

*"Once she stopped rushing
through life,
she was amazed
how much more life she had
time for."*

*– unknown*

# Chapter 20: Creating Time For SLOW

The last few days leading up to and beginning a new school year virtually in the fall of 2020 were a sort of epiphany for me. You see, they came on the heels of the MOST FULL week I have felt in a long time. The most stress, the most to-dos, the most exhausted-to-the-point-of-tears almost everyday weeks I can remember. These weeks were rushed with crossing off of lists to just make it through each day. I wasn't kind to the people I love most. I wasn't intentional. I was just existing from one day to the next. I moved through lists just to find a means to an end, and I hated it. I loathed that I was going through the day just to get through it.

To be honest, I really can't think of a worse thing. Moving through life just to get through it - what's the point?

I know its cliché, but this life really is too short. I don't want to wish a minute of it away. I LOVE the people I get to live it with: my family, close friends and coworkers that I genuinely enjoy and respect. Not to mention, our kids are growing up way too fast, and soon the small moments with them on the couch after dinner watching old reruns of *Parks and Rec* will be over. I am realizing that in the midst of loading up the calendar again with dance lessons, dentist appointments, and now a massive amount of Zoom meetings, I need to schedule time for slow, present and engaged.

2020 was anything but usual. In a year of a pandemic we were thrown curveball after curveball. But, what I think we have been given, up until this point, is the gift of slow. And now as things ramp up in a whole new way, I need to remember what I learned by being forced to stay home.

I need to make time and, if necessary, schedule in the SLOW.

Thinking back to one of my blog posts on self-care... What are the things in my life right now that bring me peace and joy and calm?

Well for me, they are movie nights on the couch with my family, conversations with my son in the car, going on a run with my daughter in the crisp fall air, or catching up with my hubby first thing in the morning over a cup of coffee before things get busy.

You see, these things are what bring me the most JOY and keep me going when things are hectic - even in the crazy unknown of this new virtual/hybrid/in-person school experience.

This season needs to be a time for more slow. More present. More engaged.

So, I am going to vow to myself to sprinkle joy in as much as possible and not go back to my "hamster wheel" life. Even if I have to get up earlier to have a cup of coffee alone with my latest book or squeeze in a quick coffee date/conversation in the car with my teenager on the way to the next event.

What if we didn't rush through this season as a list of what we need to cross off? What if we sprinkled in all the good stuff that we love in the cracks of the busy? I don't know about you, but those moments filled with the things I love give me energy and fill my heart with all that I need to power through the lists. What if we did more of that? I can't help but think we just might be happier people because of it.

# Action Step:

This week I challenge you to schedule in slow at least 3 times. Make time for that phone call, that conversation, that connection that lifts you up, and not only keeps you going, but makes your life richer.

# Reflect!

Three times I will add SLOW to my life this week are...

1. _____

2. _____

3. _____

*"Take Time to do
What Makes Your Soul Happy."*

*— unknown*

# Chapter 21: Life Changing Personalized Self-Care

E VERYWHERE you go self-care is plastered on everything! Every other social media post contains these buzzwords!

With our new normal of teaching students at school and online while monitoring our own kids at home, and learning it all as we go, it's no wonder all you hear is "Go pamper yourself, you deserve it!"

And, you know, you probably do!

BUT when the words self-care come out of our mouths, it feels exactly like a free pass to go spend exuberant amounts of money getting manicures, pedicures and massages. Not to mention retail therapy buying all the things you don't really need to make you feel happy inside.

The fact is, I have absolutely enjoyed every-single-minute of each of these activities. BUT it's afterward that I still feel the same way I did going in. (Only with pretty nails)

I struggle with the fact that, after I finally go and get these services, even though I enjoy them, I am right back to where I started - feeling overwhelmed and exhausted.

Why is this? Do you ever feel this way?

I've come to the conclusion that manicures and pedicures don't solve anything that's going on in my head OR make my life easier.

Self-care, I am learning, has nothing to do with occasional pampering and EVERYTHING to do with creating a lifestyle that allows for rest and enjoyment not occasionally, but often.

Here's how I personalize my own self-care and how you can make it a perfect fit for your lifestyle:

First, take a look at this past year in your calendar. Comb through month by month, week by week, and day by day. Review all of the events that took place in your life. Make a list of what worked, what didn't, what you want more of, and what you want less of.

Then zero-in on the things you really LOVED and want to do more of. Circle your top 5.

*For example, activities that I love are long runs, date nights (or really any date with my hubby, even if it is to get the car serviced), coffee dates with my girlfriends, a good book and a bath, and movie nights with our kids. These things bring me the utmost contentment and joy. I feel relaxed, at peace, and the most myself when doing these things. They fill my heart and help me to rest and decompress.*

# My Life This Year

| Things I **LOVED** | Things I **didn't Love** |
| --- | --- |
| _____ | _____ |
| _____ | _____ |
| _____ | _____ |
| _____ | _____ |
| _____ | _____ |
| _____ | _____ |
| _____ | _____ |
| _____ | _____ |
| _____ | _____ |
| _____ | _____ |
| _____ | _____ |

Now, add to the list of Things You Loved about this year and create your own personalized list. THIS list is what you need to add to your calendar, **liberally**! Sprinkle them in more and more. As you do this, you will become more intentional about true self-care until it becomes a habit and you become happier.

You see, these are things you truly love, and they may not cost a thing. You can do them as often as you like. AND...You are more likely to schedule them in because you look forward to doing them, and they are not a burden. The truth is, by doing these things, everything else will become easier because you are building in time to decompress by doing activities you truly enjoy, which is the ultimate, most personalized form of self-care.

## Action Steps:

1.  Pull up your calendar from the last year and begin to look through all of the things you did that you absolutely loved.

2.  Spend a few minutes jotting them down and reflecting on the people you were with and how you enjoyed that time.

3.  Now act! Slide them into your calendar as much as possible. This type of self-care will continually give back and help you to feel more rested and rejuvenated as you conquer the tasks of everyday life.

# *Reflect!*

I will set aside time to look through my calendar and begin to add more of what makes me happy on this day at this time.

Day _____ Time _____

By adding more of what I love into my life, I feel _____

_____

_____

_____

_____

_____

*"Be the Reason Someone Smiles.
Be the Reason Someone Feels Loved
and
Believes in the Goodness of
People."*

*– Roy T. Bennett*

# Chapter 22: Finding Joy by Connecting With Others

Do you ever think of someone and comment in your head, "I should call them."

Does someone just pop into your head for no reason at all?

Do you drive through a familiar place and just think of a person or group of people?

The answer is WE ALL DO.

We are constantly thinking of others. Whether it be a memory or time of day that triggers that person in your mind, you are thinking of them.

So what do we do with our thoughts?

Let's be honest. Most of the time we dismiss them. We let them go and move about our day never to hear from them again.

But what if we change that. What if we act on those thoughts? What if we reach out in a real, authentic, raw way?

*Last weekend, I was running errands. My list was long and I was on a mission. But as I passed by Albertson's grocery store, I thought of my dad. He LOVES the grocery store. He goes almost every day. He is always looking for that great bargain, but I swear he gets the most enjoyment out of socializing with the employees.*

*So at my next stop, before getting out of the car, I sent dad a quick text. **Hey dad, thinking of you! Hope you have a great day.** Of course, I got a phone call back, like I always do. We chatted for a minute and then went about our day just a little bit happier than before.*

You see, it is WAY easier than you think. It will lift your mood, lift the mood of the person you connect with, AND build your relationship with that person. Who doesn't want that?

So here is a challenge for you this week: I want you to ACT...every time someone pops into your head. YES...Every. Time.

Here's HOW:

Every time you think of someone... maybe their mom is in the hospital, or they are struggling with kids at home, or life is just hard right now...

Shoot them a TEXT.

If they're getting ready for a really big test or a big job interview...

Send off a quick TEXT.

If they pop into your mind for NO REASON AT ALL...

Type a few words and click SEND!

It doesn't have to be long or lengthy or full of details. Just a **Thinking of You**, or **Good Luck Today** or **Way to Go** or **Can't wait to hear all about it** can go a LONG way.

I know I love it when people think of me and show they care. BUT I also know that showing you care about someone feels EVEN BETTER!

Not only are you creating joy for someone else, you are creating joy for yourself!

## Action Step:

Today! The minute someone pops into your head, shoot them a text. Don't dismiss it. Let your text be this simple... **Thinking of you today. Hope you are having a great day. OR You popped into my head today. Hope you are having a great day.** You have no idea the impact you will have with just a few simple words.

# *Reflect!*

Who immediately comes to mind and how are you going to reach out to them? _____

_____

_____

_____

_____

_____

_____

How did it make you feel after you reached out?

_____

_____

_____

_____

_____

*"There is Always that One*
*Summer*
*that Changes You."*

*– unknown*

# Chapter 23: Organize Your Summer in 3 Easy Steps

How to lay it all out so that you have time for everything (and nothing at all)!

Have you ever been so excited for summer to begin? Do you think that you are finally going to have some TIME to get things done? If you are anything like me, your head is filled with grandiose plans to reorganize cabinets, restructure meal plans, purge unwanted items, take on small projects around the house and, of course, rest and play.

But then...

It seems that glorious summer somehow slips through your fingers. The days fly by and you end up at the beginning of the school year, yet again, with no progress made. Closets are still full, projects are still undone, and you really don't even remember what you were thinking about 2 months ago when the school year ended.

This was ME... for the longest time. I would get a few things done, but always felt scattered. I would wake up asking myself what to do today? I'd move from thing to thing, here and there, and go weeks without doing any of it. Until a couple of years ago while listening again to teacher-author, Angela Watson, I discovered a WHOLE NEW SYSTEM for conquering summer... and I haven't looked back since.

Here's how I do it from start to finish so you can include everything you want to get done and still have time to rest and relax with those you love.

# Step 1 - Brain Dump:

Write everything down that you want to get done by the end of summer in these areas:

- ★ Home
- ★ Work
- ★ Family
- ★ Self-Care

I just bullet them out, but get them ALL down. (It's okay if this takes a couple of days.) I have included a template for you to use on the next page.

## Summer Brain Dump

| Home | Work |
|------|------|
| Family | Self-Care |

**Step 2 - Big Ideas:**

Look at your planner and give yourself a goal for each week. I write it in the Sunday section. It could be appointments, closet clean out, meal plan, or any variety of home projects. Make sure to include vacation and dates with friends and your spouse. If you have to schedule in time for yourself. DO IT!

Make sure to group **like items together** to make the most of your time. (For example, I might include all appointments in one week or pair cleaning out closets with a yard sale.)

I have included month-at-a-glance calendars for your summer work.

*Summer plans* for the month of _____

| Sunday | Monday | Tuesday | Wednesday | Thursday | Friday | Saturday |
|--------|--------|---------|-----------|----------|--------|----------|
|        |        |         |           |          |        |          |
|        |        |         |           |          |        |          |
|        |        |         |           |          |        |          |
|        |        |         |           |          |        |          |
|        |        |         |           |          |        |          |

*Summer plans* for the month of _____

| Sunday | Monday | Tuesday | Wednesday | Thursday | Friday | Saturday |
|--------|--------|---------|-----------|----------|--------|----------|
|        |        |         |           |          |        |          |
|        |        |         |           |          |        |          |
|        |        |         |           |          |        |          |
|        |        |         |           |          |        |          |
|        |        |         |           |          |        |          |

*Summer plans* for the month of _____

| Sunday | Monday | Tuesday | Wednesday | Thursday | Friday | Saturday |
|--------|--------|---------|-----------|----------|--------|----------|
|        |        |         |           |          |        |          |
|        |        |         |           |          |        |          |
|        |        |         |           |          |        |          |
|        |        |         |           |          |        |          |
|        |        |         |           |          |        |          |

**Step 3 - Schedule Your Week:**

As you approach each week, schedule **when** you are going to do each task, day and time. For example, if you have home projects as your big idea, Monday could be purchasing items, Tuesday could be deconstruction, and Wednesday could be organizing and reassembling the finished product. This template is on my website www.thisorganizedteacherlife. com under RESOURCES so you can print out as many as you need to get you through the whole summer!

## The Week of _____

| Sunday | Monday | Tuesday | Wednesday | Thursday | Friday | Saturday |
|--------|--------|---------|-----------|----------|--------|----------|
| 5am | 5am | 5am | 5am | 5am | 5am | 5am |
| 6am | 6am | 6am | 6am | 6am | 6am | 6am |
| 7am | 7am | 7am | 7am | 7am | 7am | 7am |
| 8am | 8am | 8am | 8am | 8am | 8am | 8am |
| 9am | 9am | 9am | 9am | 9am | 9am | 9am |
| 10am | 10am | 10am | 10am | 10am | 10am | 10am |
| 11am | 11am | 11am | 11am | 11am | 11am | 11am |
| 12pm | 12pm | 12pm | 12pm | 12pm | 12pm | 12pm |
| 1pm | 1pm | 1pm | 1pm | 1pm | 1pm | 1pm |
| 2pm | 2pm | 2pm | 2pm | 2pm | 2pm | 2pm |
| 3pm | 3pm | 3pm | 3pm | 3pm | 3pm | 3pm |
| 4pm | 4pm | 4pm | 4pm | 4pm | 4pm | 4pm |
| 5pm | 5pm | 5pm | 5pm | 5pm | 5pm | 5pm |
| 6pm | 6pm | 6pm | 6pm | 6pm | 6pm | 6pm |
| 7pm | 7pm | 7pm | 7pm | 7pm | 7pm | 7pm |
| 8pm | 8pm | 8pm | 8pm | 8pm | 8pm | 8pm |
| 9pm | 9pm | 9pm | 9pm | 9pm | 9pm | 9pm |
| 10pm | 10pm | 10pm | 10pm | 10pm | 10pm | 10pm |

That's it!

This system really helps me zero-in on what I want to do over the course of the summer. It helps me stay focused on what I need to get done, but more importantly, it helps me to relax because I know what needs to get done will get done and I can rest without the guilt.

## Action Steps:

1.  Brain Dump! Spend the next few days thinking about all you want to get done this summer. As you think of it, add it to the proper section on the Brain Dump page. It's important that you take your time with this step and that you actually begin.

2.  Then, when you're ready, move through the next two steps. You'll be shocked at just how much you accomplish this summer and with so much less stress because you have thought about it and planned it out.

## *Reflect!*

This week I will take time to plan out my summer on _____ at _____ .

After I planned out my summer, I felt _____

_____

_____

_____

_____

_____

_____

"*Set goals
that excite and scare you
at the same time.*"

*–unknown*

# Chapter 24: Creating a ONE Word Goal for the New Year

E very year as we head into the New Year, I can't help but think there are many THINGS I would love to improve in my life.

Traditionally, I make a long list of resolutions I want to attack the entire year and then spend the entire month, ok maybe the first 2 weeks (let's be real) of January focusing diligently on that.

Amped up workouts, liquid diets, cleaned out closets, organized clutter. All of these THINGS sound great!! ...and IF I accomplish them, even better!

But here's the thing... if I complete these tasks, I get to cross them off my list, I get to feel that sense of immediate gratification, BUT is THAT what I am really trying to accomplish here? ....maybe.

But maybe not.

Maybe I want just a little bit more.

Maybe I want this year to be a year of continual change and continual growth for me as a whole person.

Maybe this year I want it to look different.

This year I'm going to choose ONE WORD that I will focus on to be the guiding light of my year. This one word will encompass how I want to approach a new year in work, relationships, and spiritual life. This word will be in the constant forefront of my thoughts, my plans, but most importantly, my actions for the New Year. This word will require discipline and full effort if it is who I desire to be by the end of the year.

Finding this word starts by looking inside and really examining myself to find what I REALLY want out of my life this year. This is a word that I have prayed about. A word that will propel me forward. A word that has meaning and abundance and makes me excited and nervous all in the same breath.

This year, my word is BRAVE.

This year I will reach a little further than I ever have before. I will listen and learn and leap. I will find comfort in the uncomfortable and strive to get a little bit closer to what I was put on this earth to do.

I am excited to get to know you better. I am excited to dig deep and connect and learn more about the people around me. I am ecstatic about this year and all of its possibility and I can't wait to get started.

What about you? What word will you choose?

## Action Steps:

1. Take a minute and look inward. What do you want from this year? How would you like to see yourself at the end of the year? Ask yourself these questions and reflect on WHO you WANT to be. Answer with a few words using the lines provided below.

_____

_____

_____

_____

_____

_____

_____

_____

_____

_____

_____

_____

_____

_____

2. Brainstorm all of your options. I have given you a few ideas below.

| | | |
|---|---|---|
| -Driven | -Leap | -Consistent |
| -Strength | -Determination | -Unstoppable |
| -Strong | -Forgiving | -Committed |
| -Radiant | -Free | -Organized |
| -Believe | -Dependable | -Grow |
| -Doer | -Self-Acceptance | -Momentum |
| -Courage | -Less | -Forward |
| -Boldness | -Transformational | -Brave |
| -Wholehearted | -Intentional | -Simplify |
| -Daring | -Finisher | -Mindful |
| -Progress | -Power | -Bloom |

Write down 5 that you like. 5 that speak to you.

_____

_____

_____

_____

_____

3. Narrow your options! Think about and visualize those words. I let them bounce around in my head for a few days. Think about them, pray about them, and visualize them. Then pick ONE!

4. Now SHARE! Tell people your word! Not only do you hear it and think about it, but by telling others, they will hold you accountable. They will ask you about it, and you can share how you are growing and changing because of your word!

# *Reflect!*

What changes have you made or have planned to make over the course of this book? Which ones do you plan to keep and why? _____

_____

_____

_____

_____

_____

_____

_____

_____

_____

_____

_____

_____

_____

_____

_____

_____

_____

_____

_____

_____

_____

_____

_____

*Cheers* to you, for finishing this book!

*Cheers* to small, impactful changes made over time.

*Cheers* to a happier, healthier, teacher.

Know that I am cheering you on the whole way!

# Works Cited

Burchard, B. (2014, August 17). From https://www.youtube.com/watch?v=v2mY36Ho1Sk

Burchard, B. (n.d.). *The Brendon Show*. From Brendon.com: https://brendon.com/podcast/

Hatmaker, J. (n.d.). *Jen Hatmaker*. From For the Love Podcast: https://jenhatmaker.com/podcast/

Hollis, R. (n.d.). *Hollis Co*. From The Rachel Hollis Podcast: https://thehollisco.com/blogs/rachel-hollis-podcast

Smith, A. (n.d.). *Strategies*. From This Organized Teacher Life: https://thisorganizedteacherlife.com/

Watson, A. (2016). *The Cornerstone for Teachers*. From The 40 Hour Teacher Workweek Club: www.thecornerstoneforteachers.com

Watson, A. (n.d.). *The Truth for Teachers Podcast*. From https://thecornerstoneforteachers.com/truth-for-teachers-podcast/